You're A Brave Man, Charlie Brown

YOU'RE A BRAVE MAN, CHARLIE BROWN

Selected Cartoons from
You Can Do It, Charlie Brown,
Vol. II

by Charles M. Schulz

FAWCETT CREST • NEW YORK

A Fawcett Crest Book
Published by Ballantine Books

Contents: Peanuts ® comic strip by Charles M. Schulz
Copyright © 1963 by United Feature Syndicate, Inc.

ISBN 0-449-21058-8

This book comprises the second half of You Can Do It,
Charlie Brown and is reprinted by arrangement with Holt,
Rinehart and Winston, Inc.

Printed in Canada

First Fawcett Crest Edition: November 1969
First Ballantine Books Edition: November 1985

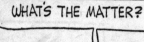

WHAT AM I GOING TO DO, CHARLIE BROWN?

MY "BLANKET-HATING" GRANDMA IS COMING TO VISIT US...SHE'LL BE ON ME THE FIRST THING ABOUT THIS BLANKET...SHE'LL HOUND ME TO DEATH...

SHE SAYS SHE RAISED FIVE CHILDREN OF HER OWN, AND THEY DIDN'T HAVE BLANKETS AND NO GRANDCHILD OF HERS IS GOING TO HAVE A BLANKET EITHER!

MAYBE SHE'S CALMED DOWN SINCE THE LAST TIME SHE WAS HERE...

MAYBE THE MOON WILL FALL OUT OF THE SKY!

THEIR PARENTS DON'T APPROVE
OF THEIR BEING TOGETHER...

HE THINKS IF HE SITS IN THE RAIN LOOKING PATHETIC, SOME RICH LADY WILL COME ALONG IN A BIG CAR, AND TAKE HIM TO HER HOME TO LIVE A LIFE OF EASE

WHAT SORT OF LIFE DOES HE THINK HE'S LIVING NOW?

FOR ONE THING, I'M SURROUNDED BY SARCASM!

I'VE DECIDED TO BECOME A "POLLED HEREFORD" RANCHER

LOOK...HERE'S A PICTURE OF A BULL THAT SOLD FOR OVER FOUR THOUSAND DOLLARS! ISN'T THAT TERRIFIC?

I COULD BECOME RICH! AND I WOULDN'T HAVE TO SELL VERY MANY OF THEM, EITHER..

WHY, LOOK HOW MUCH I'D MAKE IF I ONLY SOLD AS LITTLE AS ONE A DAY!

I CAN'T LET YOU IN, SNOOPY... MY MOTHER DOESN'T LIKE THE SMELL OF A WET DOG...

MY MIND REELS WITH SARCASTIC REPLIES!

IS YOUR MOTHER ENJOYING HER NEW TANGERINE POOL TABLE?

OH, YES... SHE AND HER GIRL FRIENDS HAVE A GOOD TIME.. THEY DRINK COFFEE AND PLAY POOL ALMOST EVERY MORNING...

SHE SPEAKS A WHOLE NEW LANGUAGE NOW...

LAST NIGHT SHE SAID TO ME, "GO TO BED, EIGHT-BALL!"

I'M IN TROUBLE, SNOOPY..

ALL THE KIDS ARE MAD AT ME BECAUSE THEIR MOTHERS ARE SPENDING SO MUCH TIME PLAYING POOL ON MY MOTHER'S NEW TANGERINE-COLORED POOL TABLE...

YOU WOULD NEVER THINK THAT JUST CHANGING THE COLOR OF THE CLOTH FROM GREEN TO TANGERINE WOULD MAKE SUCH A DIFFERENCE

I WONDER WHAT WOULD HAPPEN IF THEY MADE GOLF COURSES PINK!

OH, NO!

OTHER KIDS' BASEBALL HEROES HIT HOME RUNS...MINE GETS SENT DOWN TO THE MINORS!

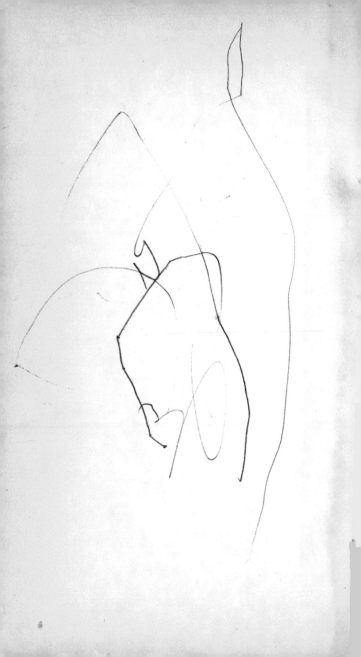